Also by the same author
Mostly Love Poems,
published by Upfront Publishing in 2002

MORE LOVE POEMS

Stuart Mallinson

UPFRONT PUBLISHING
LEICESTERSHIRE

MORE LOVE POEMS
Copyright © Stuart Mallinson 2003

All Rights Reserved

No part of this book may be reproduced in any form
by photocopying or by any electronic or mechanical means,
including information storage or retrieval systems,
without permission in writing from both the copyright
owner and the publisher of this book.

ISBN 1-84426-232-4

First Published 2003 by
UPFRONT PUBLISHING LTD
Leicestershire

Printed by Lightning Source

MORE LOVE POEMS

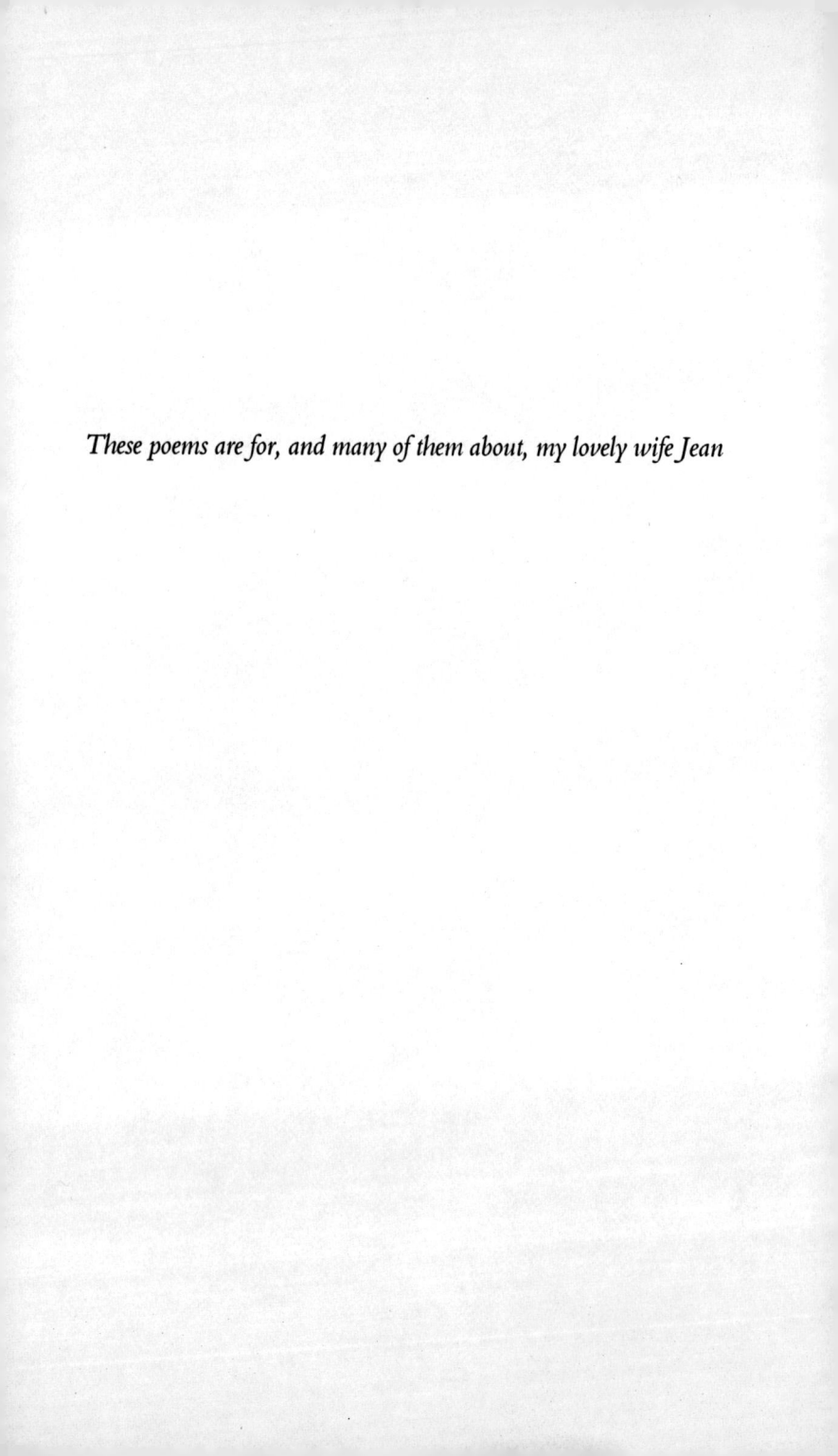

These poems are for, and many of them about, my lovely wife Jean

Foreword

This book, again, contains mostly love poems, although there are a few others. The last section is 'Poems for the POU'. This is the Pulmonary Oncology Unit, the Lung Cancer Unit, at Wythenshawe Hospital, Manchester, which Jean attended for nearly two years. In this place, there is great love, compassion, hard work, heartbreak, and sometimes humour. I was privileged to meet and know patients and staff there.

Stuart Mallinson 2003

Contents

Foreword	7
I Remember	12
When You Are Near	13
I Know	14
My Theme	15
Gather Ye Rosebuds	17
Wild Flowers	18
Love at First Sight	19
A Star	20
FCU 3612	21
The Nudists	23
Give In	24
Christmas 1952	25
Dresses	27
The Wooden Bridge at Grasmere	29
To Nuzzle	30
Where You Would Stop and See	31
In Aberdeenshire	32
On a Lack of Inspiration	33
Sorrento	35
Valentine	40
Alone on a Chair	41
We Never Did	43
Did the Earth Move?	44
Forgive Me	45
Watendlath	47
Home	49
Carr Hill Road	51
Lady in Red	52
Sit Upon My Knee	53
Buchan	55
No Space Between	56

On Losing My Job	57
Gorgeous	59
On Iraq	60
The Glory of the Battle	61
I Need Yer	63
A Poor Sort of Man 1	64
A Poor Sort of Man 2	65
Time's Gone By, Lad	66
Roots	67
And the Company Pays	68
Going Back From Leave	69
To Jean	71
Sundays Apart in 1953	72
Missing You	73
Cooking	74
Unusual?	75
Union Street, Aberdeen	76
Andalucia	77
Poems for the POU	79
The POU	80
The POU	81
Hope	82
The Board at the POU	83
Lanzarote	85
Bill	86
Remember You Are Mine	87
Gemcitabine	88
Lamb Chops	90
The Bed	91
An Inspiration	92
The Corridor	93
The Waiting Room	94
Moira	95
Winter	98
Time	99
Our Time	100
If You Go Away	101
Waiting	102

The Defining Moment	103
1953 and 2002	105
The Dragonfly	106
With You	107
I Am With You	109

And I remember eyes of blue,
And, oh, the joy, of loving you

When You Are Near

When you are with your heart's desire
Everything has new attire.
Ordinary things now brighter look,
Like coloured pages from a book,
The sun's rays now brighter shine,
At the very thought that you are mine.
All around, the countryside
Is fair and lovely for my bride.
The birds sing louder, and the air
Is still and fragrant with you there.
The night is velvet, and the moon
With your sweet beauty is in tune
      When you are near, my heart's on fire
      Everything has new attire.

I Know

I don't care what others think,
I know.
I know the truth from which they shrink,
Just so.
I know what matters, and does not,
In this life of high and low,
I know what matters to us all,
Each mountain climb, and each fall,
Oh yes, I know.

You might think a little wealth
Would help to smooth the way.
Or some kind of guarantee of health,
To give a carefree day.
Some would seek a warmer clime,
An easing off of work.
Some would seek elusive fame
As perhaps the final perk.

But I tell you, these don't matter.
What does?
I really know
It's a good woman beside you,
Who says, 'I love you so.'

My Theme

Let me write a poem to you
From time to time
Put therein a word or two,
Make for you a rhyme.
In this complicated life,
It seems right to me,
A simple theme should dominate
What we have to be.

I do not find it difficult
To pen my love for you,
For it fills the whole of me,
Nothing else gets through.
All my life is dominated
By my love, it's true,
My love for you, my darling wife;
My simple theme
Is you.

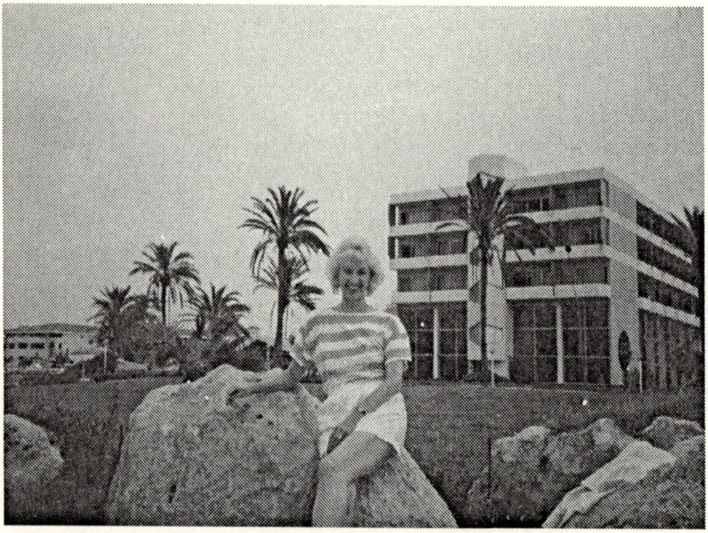

Gather Ye Rosebuds

Sitting out in the sun, near the bar,
Looking across the gardens to the beach and the sea,
Enjoying the warmth of Paphos,
And the five-star hotel,
Living it up for a fortnight, in Cyprus,
You and me.

You look like a film star sitting there,
With stripy shorts, bikini top, and your sunglasses,
Enjoying the Mediterranean sun,
The Imperial Beach Hotel,
Sitting here with glass in hand,
Time quickly passes.

And I am worried,
Worried because my business back home is down,
And I do not really enjoy the sun,
My mind is far from here,
Sitting with my lovely wife,
My face wearing a frown.

Your favourite saying, I know, is,
'Gather ye rosebuds while ye may,
Take that frown from off your brow,
Enjoy the here and now,
Your work will be there for you to do
Another day,
Never forget that I love you.'

Wild Flowers

Past Crosthwaite, there is a bank of snowdrops,
That we eagerly look for every year,
Telling us we've seen the last of winter,
Before any other flowers will appear.

At the side of the road that runs to Brigsteer,
There is a place where cowslips crowd the grass,
And we will drive there just to see those cowslips,
Stop, look, admire then slowly pass.

In early summer, the woods near Grasmere
Have bluebells as far as you can see.
And we will laugh, and stroll among those bluebells,
Before retiring to the village for some tea.

You love to go to Hayes, the garden centre,
On the outskirts of Ambleside,
But most of all you love the wild flowers,
That litter the Lakeland countryside.

The carpet of croci outside Hawkshead,
The daffodils beside Windermere,
The catkins, the poppies, and the heather,
These are the flowers held most dear,
And we go and seek them all, every year.

Love at First Sight

Love at first sight,
Is that the way
Relationships
Are formed today?

Do they look at each other
And then they know
That from now on
Their love will grow?

At that first moment
Can they believe
A life together will
Happiness achieve?

The truth is, no one can tell
What will their future be,
But love at first sight worked very well
When I met you, and you met me.

A Star

I open my hand
To catch a star
And there you are.

To make dreams come true
I close my eyes
And there are you

For pleasure
Let my imagination fill
I see you still.

My dream, my pleasure
And my star
My love forever
All these you are.

FCU 3612

Fighter Control Unit 3612,
RAF Dyce, thinking of you,
A letter a day,
Each week to the phone,
Ringing a call box,
To you, there back home.

Fighter Control Unit 3612,
RAF Dyce, longing for you.
Cricket and football,
Never a flight,
Panto in Aberdeen,
Singing each night.

Fighter Control Unit 3612,
RAF Dyce, how I love you,
I started my poetry
Writing to you,
I adore you my darling,
From 3612.

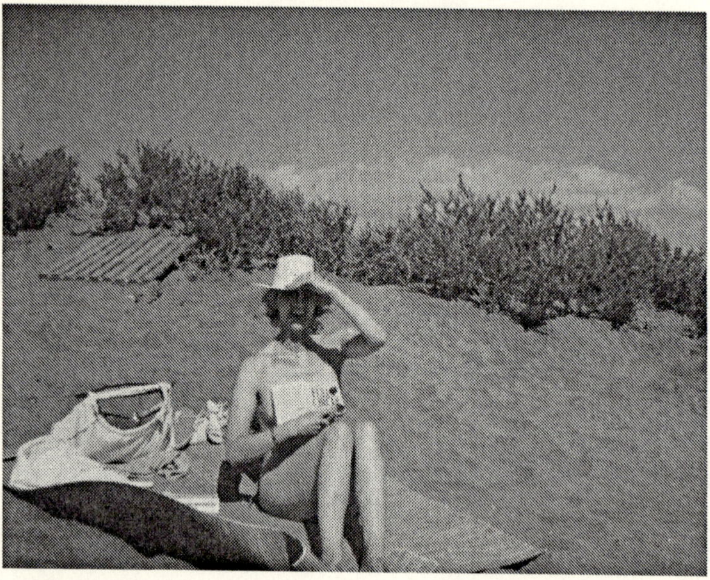

The Nudists

On the nudist beaches, on the Med,
However hard you try,
It isn't always easy
To look folks in the eye.

The first time we went to a nudist beach,
Jean looked at all the men,
And then, as if to be quite sure,
She looked at them again.
She smiled,
>'My holiday will not be marred,
>Having laid my eyes
>On all the guys,
>I hold you in high regard!'

Give In

The young doctor in Coronation Street
Had parted from his wife,
Life was one long quarrel,
One long marital strife.
He lodged with Ashley and Maxine,
Almost next to home.
Though distraught with all his troubles,
He didn't want to roam.
'We never stop fighting yet,
I commit no sin.
How do you and Maxine get on?'
Said Ashley,
'I give in.'

Christmas 1952

It was just after Christmas, 1952
We'd been to the cinema,
Our first date,
Me and you.
And afterwards we went
To my choirmaster's house,
To meet my parents, the choirmaster,
His daughter, and his spouse.

Annie was his daughter,
I'd known her for a while,
She was ten years older,
Married with a child,
But we were pals, and I asked her,
On one side, as we stood there,
'What do you think, dear Annie,
Of my girl so fair?'

So no one else could hear her,
She whispered quietly,
'I think that she is lovely,'
That's what Annie said to me.
And so you were, my darling,
As lovely as could be,
I will remember what Annie said
For always, you will see.

Annie lost her husband,
And he was only young,
Then she herself got sick and died,
At only forty-one.
But I recall her speaking,
All those years ago
The first to say 'You're lovely,'
A truth that I now know.

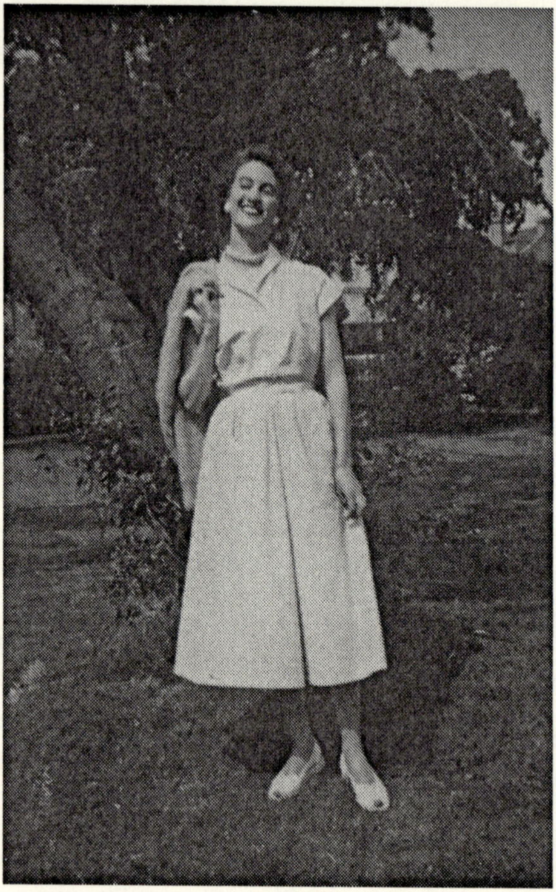

Dresses

One was a plain, lemon, yellow,
Another, striped, green and white,
A third white, with pink flowers,
Was an absolute delight.
The fourth, pink with white dots,
Was for evening wear,
And I can see you now, in each one,
Standing there.
All were summer dresses,
All had skirts flared wide,
Three-quarter length, in my memory
I see you by my side.
The year was nineteen fifty-four,
And you were twenty, and for sure,
Beautiful, elegant, and so fair,
In my mind's eye I see you there.

Our pecuniary state was very slim,
Our resources very poor,
But every penny was well spent,
For you were twenty, and for sure,
Beautiful, elegant, and so fair,
I still can see you standing there,
Back then in nineteen fifty-four.

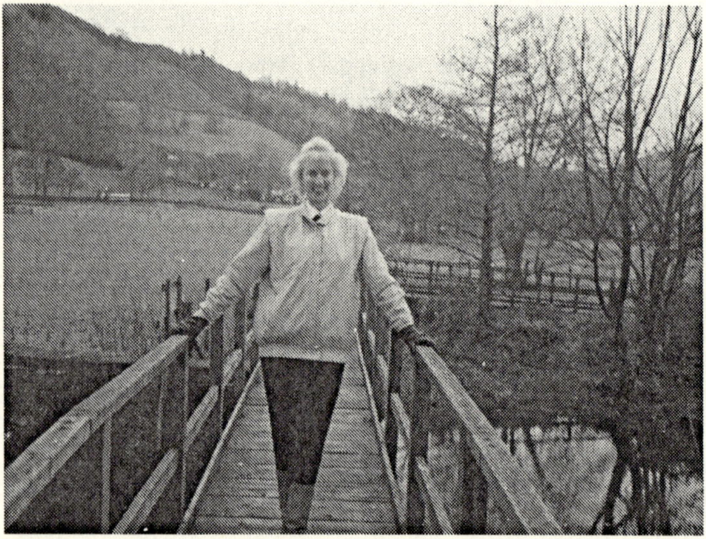

The Wooden Bridge at Grasmere

There's a wooden bridge at Grasmere,
Where the river flows fast below,
On its way to Grasmere lake,
A place that we all know.
This wooden bridge at Grasmere
Is where the village footpath goes,
Past the back of the Wordsworth Hotel,
Where the shallow river flows.
So many times have you and I
Done this little walk,
In beautiful surroundings,
We loved to stroll and talk.
The wooden bridge at Grasmere,
What memories it brings me,
Right now I see you standing there,
In all England, a place more fair,
Would be very hard to see.
> You there with me, nothing displaces
> Those memories of lovely places.

To Nuzzle

I am not at all sure what
'nuzzle' means.
Except, it means, perhaps, standing behind you,
Holding you so very close,
My face in your hair,
Sliding down and kissing your cheek,
Gently holding your breasts,
And you,
Pressing your body against mine,
Holding your face up towards mine,
'Nuzzling'
Just being totally and utterly in love.

Where You Would Stop and See

I have been writing poetry to you, for many, many years
It started in 1953.
I would leave them on your pillow, or on the bathroom mirror
Somewhere where you would perchance be,
Somewhere where you would stop and see.

I loved to see your face light up when you saw my rhyme
And you would come to me
And kiss me, and say how lovely those words were;
Words which were about just you and me
Placed somewhere where you would stop and see.

As well as poems I would write you letters
Put there for you to read and then
Come into the study, stand behind me, and then hug me,
So happy at the words that I did pen –
Why can't we have those lovely times again?

In Aberdeenshire

When I see the hillside heather,
And the mountain slopes of pine,
Or the raging, rushing, river,
Or the storm clouds in a line,
When I see the sun above me
Glorify the countryside,
Or the snowflakes gently falling,
Or the cliffs, the sea, the tide
Incoming o'er the pebbles,
Seagulls squawking in the air,
Everything there is around me
Which is beautiful and fair,
All these things remind me of you,
The way you talk, the way you kiss,
Your loveliness in every way,
Your very presence which I miss,
The lovely times we've had together,
The places that we've seen and known,
But above all these I cherish
The promise
That you'll be my own.

On a Lack of Inspiration

Can't think of another verse tonight,
At least, not one that sounds quite right,
So I'll just say that I love you,
It's true! it's true! it's true!
It's true!

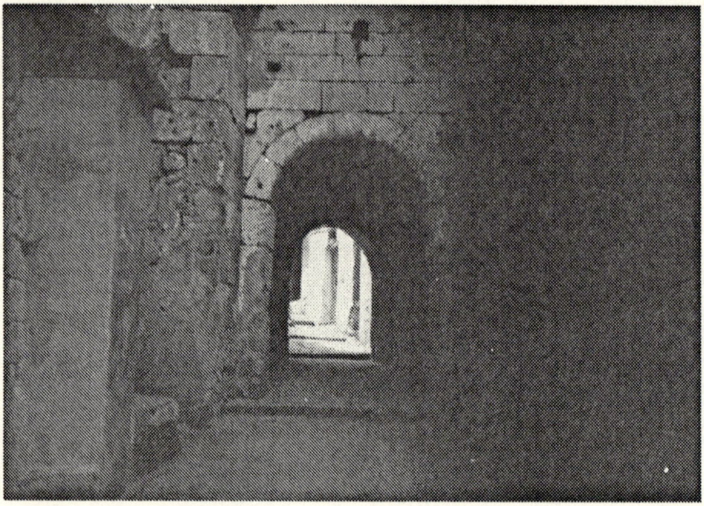

Sorrento

This is the old Greek gate
That goes back through the ages,
Long, long before we were here,
Or history turned its pages.

From our hotel, Capodimonte,
We look across Sorrento Bay,
This is the nicest place we know,
We enjoy every day.

And now we climb Vesuvius,
Mountain of ash still burning,
And walk all around Pompeii,
Where time's no longer turning.

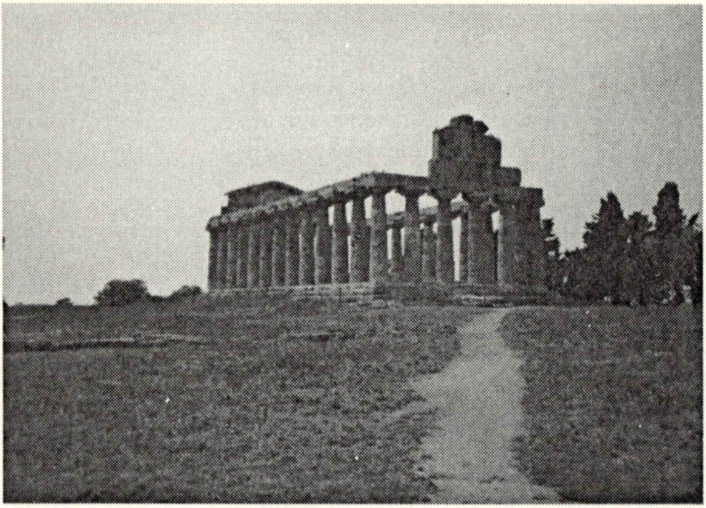

And these are the temples of Paestum,
Back to the Greeks we trace,
They are so very, very old,
This is your favourite place.

And now we're at Monte Casino,
The monastery on the hill.
Rebuilt since destruction in World War II,
When soldiers came to kill.

We see here the fishermen's nets,
Strung across the river,
The water buffalo are grazing,
A snake makes you gasp and shiver.

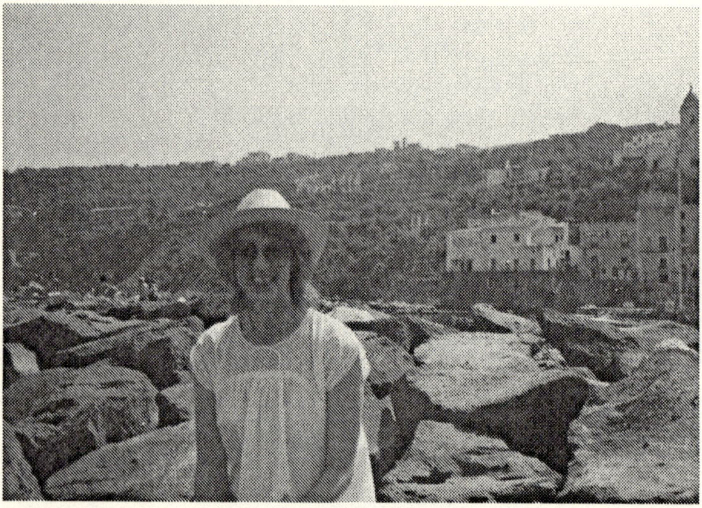

And this is you near Sorrento,
So beautiful, and moreover,
It's wonderful to be here with you,
    My cup of love runneth over.

Valentine

This valentine card is the thirty-second,
Since on the dance floor you first beckoned,
It's sent again to tell you this,
There's nothing lovelier than your kiss,
Whatever's wrong, there's no alarms
When you are close within my arms.
Although I'm telling nothing new,
My darling wife, I do love you.

Alone on a Chair

She was sitting on a chair at the side of the floor
I hadn't seen her unaccompanied before
Usually dancing in taffeta skirt
Eyes flashing, and smiling, a nose that was pert
Shoulders so straight, a blouse of snow white
Where was her regular partner tonight?

I had really no doubts, to me she looked stunning
If I didn't move fast, someone else would come running
I quickly jumped up from the girl at my side
Made my excuses, my feelings to hide
Then rapidly moved to this vision so fair
There by the dance floor, alone on a chair.

We chatted awhile, then danced all the night
Her beauty and closeness filled me with delight
She was eighteen and lovely, and I, twenty-one
We didn't know then what we had begun
We walked home together, it was getting quite late
I held her and kissed her at her garden gate.

Two years later and she was my wife
She would be with me the rest of my life
Don't ever stop saying 'I love you,'
She said to me then, and it's perfectly true
I never did
And each night said a prayer
Of thanks for the time she was alone on a chair.

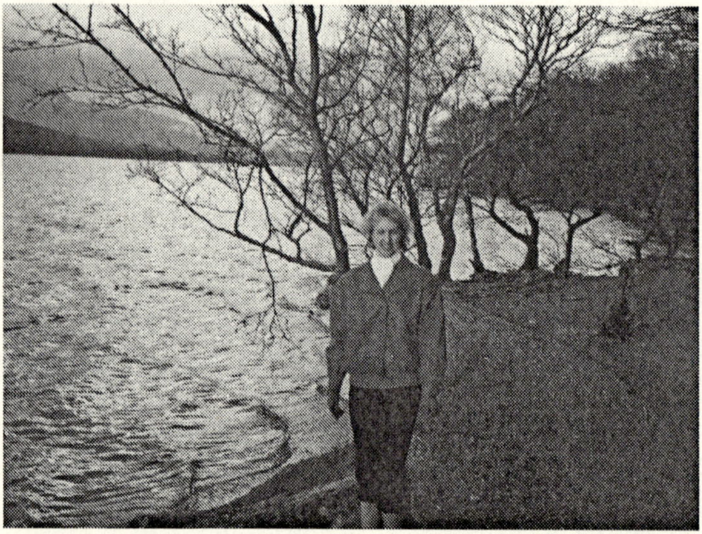

We Never Did

It was on the east side of Coniston,
Where the road runs near the lake
Quieter than the Torver road,
A pleasant route to take.
The first time that we went this way
It was a chilly winter's day.

We'll come back when the summer comes
An effort we will make,
We'll bring a book, sit peacefully,
By the road that's near the lake.
It's not too far from Windermere,
To bring a book, and sit right here.

The road to the east of Coniston,
Where you can see the odd steamboat
Goes on to Spark Bridge, and the coast,
Past the house where Ruskin wrote
To that spot among the trees, where the lake is hid,
We said we'd go and take a book,
                                      But we never did.

Did the Earth Move?

Gorgeous lady,
My sweet love,
Was that good?
Did the earth move?

Lie in my arms,
Don't dare rove,
Hold me so close,
Did the earth move?

You are my angel,
You are my dove,
This is just heaven,
Did the earth move?

I've been up volcanoes
Near tornadoes too,
Nothing was ever like
Being with you,

You bring me ecstasy,
You are my love,
You are just wonderful,
Did the earth move?

Forgive Me

I stop the car in a lay-by, near a call box,
And hurry to ring you back at home,
Already regretting my stupid temper,
Hoping, anxiously, that you'll come to the phone.
You do, and the words come pouring from me,
'I'm so sorry for the dreadful things I said,
How could I say those words which are so hurtful?
I must be crazy, daft, wrong in the head!
You know I love you so, my darling,
You are more than all the world to me,
I cannot live my life without you,
Please forgive my silly frailty.'
You answer in a voice low and even,
'I have heard the words that you have said.
Forget this morning, for I love you,
And will see you tonight, my dear.
– in bed!'

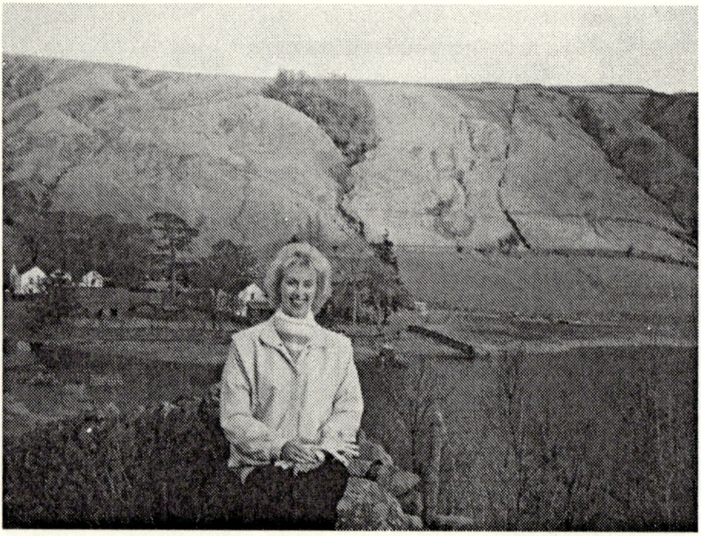

Watendlath

Judith Paris lived here,
In Hugh Walpole's book
In his chronicles of Herries,
If you care to look.

I first went to Watendlath
When a boy of ten,
And fifteen more years passed
Ere I returned again.

Then you and I, just married,
By Derwentwater stayed,
One hot afternoon, past Ladore Falls,
Through the woods, our way we made.

Over to Watendlath,
By the tarn, sat in the sun,
In that most tranquil spot we knew,
A love affair was begun.

Many years now have passed
Since we first went there,
We kept going back to Watendlath,
Maintained our love affair.

In my mind's eye I see you,
Sat there in the sun,
A much greater love affair for me
Already had begun.

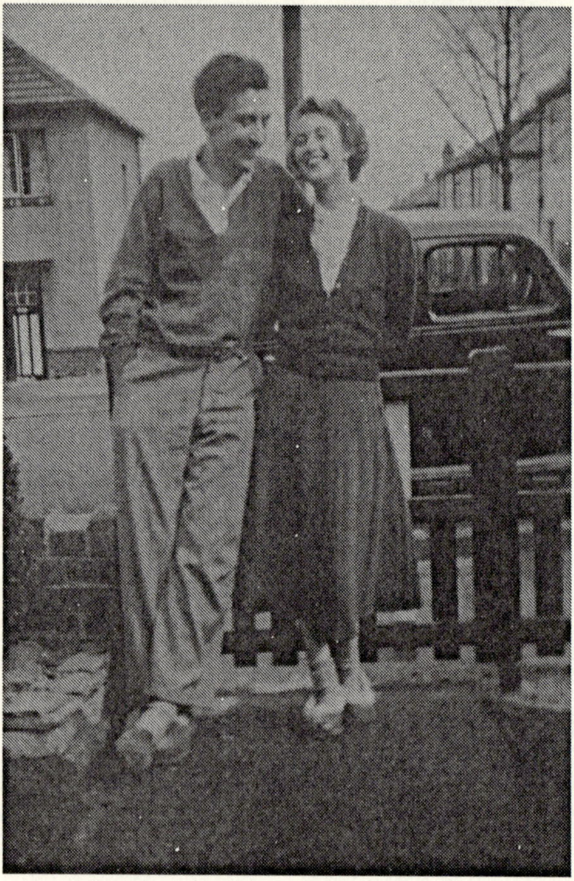

Home

It was hardly Buckingham Palace,
Or Chatsworth, or Blenheim,
It was only a two-bedroomed semi,
But for us it was a dream.
        And if I may be more precise,
        It represented paradise.

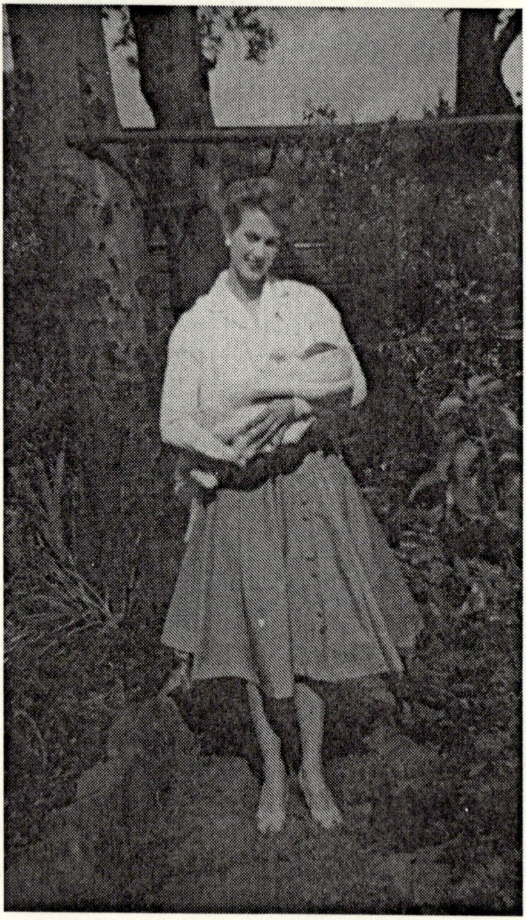

Carr Hill Road

As I walked along Carr Hill Road
To number fifty-nine,
I saw, standing in the garden
The young lady who was mine.
July was hot and sunny,
She was out there on the lawn,
Showing off her big, fat, tummy,
Awaiting our first-born.
As I walked along Carr Hill Road,
I saw her standing there,
A hosepipe held in her hand,
In her smart maternity wear.
A turquoise skirt and jacket,
White blouse with turquoise dots.
My goodness, how I loved her –
Lots and lots and lots.
As I walked along Carr Hill Road
It was very plain to me,
The great riches that I possessed
Were there for all to see.
       I walked on to number fifty-nine,
       Just thanking God that she was mine.

*The Entertainer at the
Okeanis Hotel in Rhodes
played 'Lady in Red' as
we danced around*

Lady in red, with eyes so blue
Please understand that I love you.

Lady in green, with hair so fair
Wherever you are, my heart is there.

Lady in yellow, and pink and white,
Over my being you cast a light.

Time will not change my feelings for you,
Oh, how I love my Lady in blue.

Sit Upon My Knee

You have bathed, and are standing,
Before the bathroom mirror,
Without clothes, with your back to me,
And I am sitting on the bed,
Without clothes,
Appreciating the view,
'Come and sit upon my knee.'

You come,
And my hand slips down behind you,
You reach down,
And you're gently holding me,
And we just sit there,
In absolute happiness,
You, upon my knee.

Close, and full of love,
You sit there, on my knee.
Wishing such moments never ended,
Just you, my lovely wife, and me.

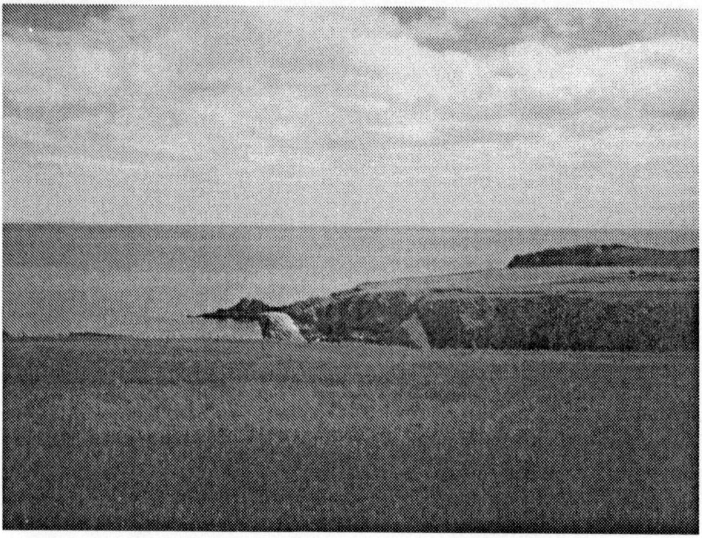

Buchan

It was like playing cowboys and Indians,
And we took it light-heartedly,
But we had our rifles (with no bullets!)
And instructions were given repeatedly,
We were attacking RAF Buchan,
A radar station near Peterhead,
It all seemed a little bit pointless,
No casualties, wounded or dead!
The lorries got us there early,
It was a lovely summer's day,
Manoeuvres started at sundown,
Around were the cliffs where we lay.
>And I looked out across the North Sea,
>And I thought of you,
>Loving, pining, aching, remembering,
>I thought of you.

The others in the grass all around me,
Waiting for darkness to come,
And I just thought of your loving,
And longed to be with you back home.
I have remembered those cliffs near Buchan,
And that afternoon in the sun,
Remembering the love between us,
The love that had just begun.
>And I looked out across the North Sea,
>And I thought of you
>Loving, pining, aching, remembering,
>I thought of you.

Two years ago I returned,
The radar station is still there,
And my mind went back nearly fifty years,
And I thought of you, Lady Fair
>And I looked out across the North Sea
>And I thought of you
>Loving, pining, aching, remembering,
>I thought of you.

No Space Between

Jean
Whose love
Is deep within me, thrills and cheers me
Lifts my life above.

Jean
My queen
Whose lips I kiss, I hold so close
There is no space between.

Jean
Whose heart
Is all to me, will always be
We'll never part.

On Losing My Job

I rang you when I lost my job
'They're wanting someone new.'
You listened carefully before you spoke
And then said, 'I love you.'

My income had been very high
My position seemed secure,
We had a pleasant living,
Could wish for little more.
And when with bad news I'd phoned,
You could have criticised, or moaned.

Instead, your love and belief in me
Was as good as it would always be.
Always loyal, loving, true.
You said simply, 'I love you.'

It's twenty years since that day
An uncertain future before us lay
But when I was down, dear eyes of blue,
I heard you whisper, 'I love you.'

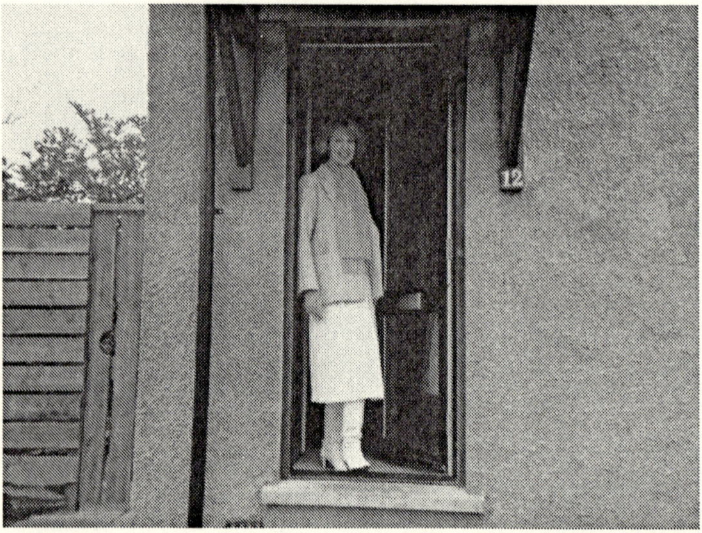
12

Gorgeous

Hiya, gorgeous!
That's what I used to say to you,
Hiya, gorgeous!
Were ever spoken words more true?

Hello, my lovely,
You look wonderful, I'd say,
It was not idle flattery,
You were like a summer's day.

You look absolutely super,
Ready to go out,
A privilege to be with you,
I want to sing and shout!

You always looked terrific,
And when I told you this,
You'd say,
'You don't look bad, yourself, you know,'
And then give me a kiss.

On Iraq

Do not fight in Iraq,
Shed so much innocent blood,
Do not fight in Iraq,
It will do no good.
It is easy to see that Bush and Blair
Have not seen service anywhere.

This is the first generation of leaders,
Who have not been under fire,
Full of sabre-rattling,
Their judgement is just dire.
On this decision let there be no takers
To support Bush and Blair, the widow-makers.

Dear God, spare
Us, not from Saddam,
But Bush and Blair

The Glory of the Battle

He sat and looked across the table
His eyes were cold and hard
As if he'd seen too many things,
His very heart was scarred.
'Don't talk to me of war,' he said,
'Or the glory of the battle,
Only an idiot would listen
To such stupid prattle.
Only a fool would consider
That war was glorious,
A fool who stayed behind the lines,
Making fools of us.'
He looked at me, his eyes were steel.
The hurt, the pain, were there to feel,
'Is ought more stupid than a battle?
Only a politician's tattle.'

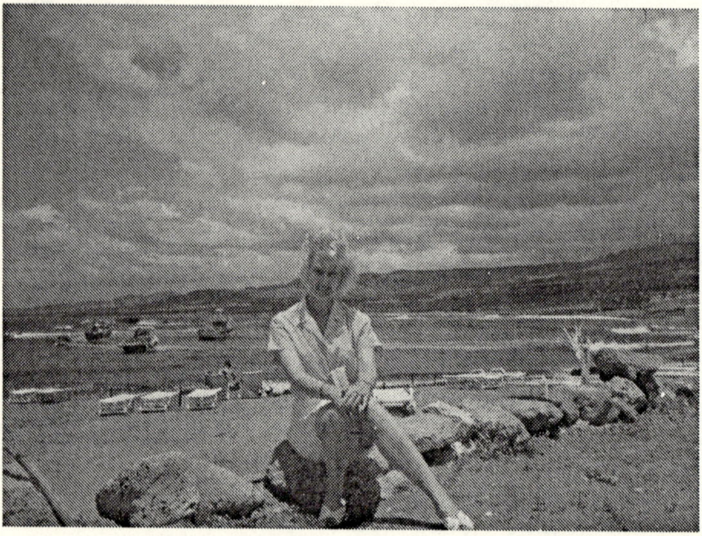

I Need Yer

All you have to do to me
Is give the slightest glance
Day and night I'm loving you
Given half a chance.

It must be some kind of bug,
I guess I've got a fever
But I certainly don't seek a cure,
You see, I'll always need yer.

At the Old England Hotel,
Bowness-on-Windermere

A Poor Sort of Man 1

'I haven't made a meal since I was wed,'
Boasted the man at the next table.
He'd be in his sixties, looked perfectly able,
I thought, *that's a stupid thing that you've just said.*

Fancy believing that was some form
Of achievement, in his self-centred world,
No wonder the flag of Women's Lib unfurled,
If men like him think that's the norm.

It's a pity no one has enlightened him,
That being wed means sharing
All the jobs, and caring,
There's no room for men like him, who are so dim.

He needs the full treatment, don't halve
Your criticisms, Oh, put-upon-wife,
Act now before he ruins your life,
Let the beggar starve!

At the Old England Hotel,
Bowness-on-Windermere

A Poor Sort of Man 2

It was time for dinner at The Old England,
And he walked towards the dining room,
His wife, finely dressed, looked beautiful,
And she walked two yards behind him, dutiful,
Like a slave, walking to her doom.

What is it with these men? You often see it,
Who always stride out before their wives,
Have they never heard of the age of chivalry?
From their nearest and dearest there is no rivalry,
Do they not know how to lead their lives?

How pleasant it is to see a man
Take his wife's hand, and let her go before,
Standing back, and making way for her,
With courtesy he must defer,
Otherwise, he's just a stupid bore.

Time's Gone By, Lad

What happened to thi mother, lad?
What happened to thi dad?
What happened to the friends tha had,
When tha warra lad?
Where are all the places
Where tha used to play?
And all the folks who stopped and talked
On the streets each day?
Are the shops still there, lad,
Where tha had to queue?
And the walk on the hill where tha used to go
That gave a lovely view?
Are the schools and playgrounds there,
Where many an hour tha spent?
And the fields and woods not far off,
Where tha used to take a tent?
What's happened to 'em all, lad,
Wherever have they gone?
Time's gone by, that's all lad,
Tha's left, the only one.

Roots

Your mother was a mender,
My mother was a weaver,
My father was a spinner,
In the dark satanic mills,
Our village was a woollen village,
The Industrial Revolution,
On the east side of the Pennine hills.

Your mother was a mender,
My mother was a weaver,
In the thirties, so long ago, they met,
My mother took me to the clinic,
Your mother took your brother,
You were not born just yet.

Your mother was a mender,
My mother was a weaver,
My father was a spinner,
Your father a shopkeeper,
In '34 you came along, we met in '52,
Oh beautiful, beautiful, daughter,
Of that mender,
That shopkeeper,
      How I love you.

And the Company Pays

I am going on the train to London,
First class, and the company pays,
And I have had breakfast in the dining car,
Expensive, but the company pays.
But now I am sitting at a table,
It is not very busy,
And I take a pad from my briefcase,
And I think of you.
And I start to compose a poem,
To you.

Sometimes, when convenient,
You have come with me,
First class, and breakfast,
And the company pays.
And you shop in the West End,
Whilst I go to meetings,
Then lunch together,
And leisurely back to Euston,
A most lovely day with you,
And the company pays.

I work hard for my company,
And the company pays.
And I adore you,
And will compose poems to you,
Forever.

Going Back From Leave

I open the parcel,
And as usual, I see,
The things that you send
With a love note for me.
The macaroons
I know you make
With an eggcup
The wrong way up,
I know the trouble that you take.
There, as usual, are the custard creams,
You know I like them, and it seems,
You do not forget,
Girl of my dreams.
Then more biscuits, buns, and cake,
I know the trouble that you take.
To Aberdeen, north, on the train,
Going back from leave again.
Though not alone, I do not speak,
I shall have this parcel next week.
      For now, you gave me another one which
      As usual, I enjoy,
      A bacon sandwich.

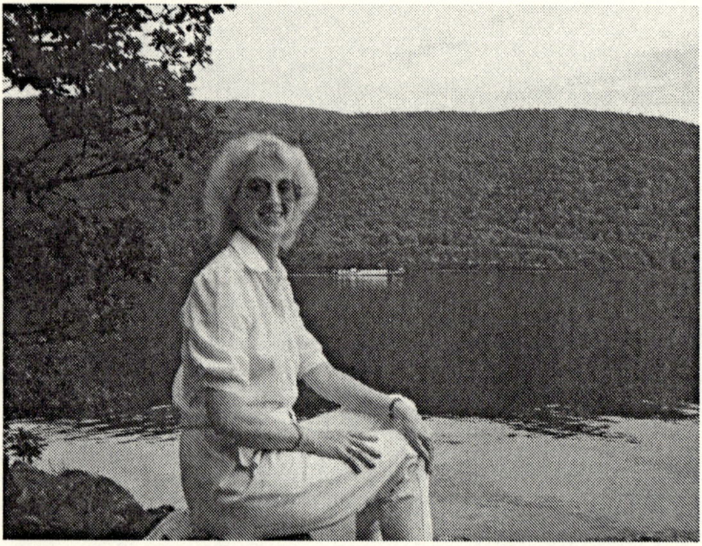

To Jean

When I am dead, say this is true,
I never loved, except for you,
Alone you occupied my heart,
It was yours right from the start,
Yours from the very day we met,
Though you are gone, it is yours yet,
When I am gone, say this is true,
I never loved except for you.

Oh, there were girls when I was young,
And boys whose praises you have sung,
But these were all just fancy-free,
Not meaningful to you or me,
I knew at once after you came,
My life would never be the same,
When I am dead, say this is true,
I never loved till I met you.

Sundays Apart in 1953

Though we are far apart, sweetheart,
We have our memories dear,
And all the bright future before us,
When these Sundays will soon be here.
For the time will pass, my darling,
Though long it may well seem,
And these happy times will come again,
Which now seem just a dream.

Missing You

I miss you like the flowers miss the sun,
Can't wait for the dark clouds to be gone,
I miss you like the flowers miss the rain,
Please let the clouds come over us again.
I miss you like the stars on a dull night,
I miss you when you are out of sight,
I miss you like good music when it's quiet,
Like a shortage of good food when on a diet.
I miss you in so many different ways,
And will continue to do so all my days.

Cooking

You asked me if I could cook,
Well, the answer is, I can.
Over the years, made many a meal,
The domesticated man.
And of course I was the number two
When Jean prepared a spread,
Made sure all the family
Were well and truly fed.
Daughter, sons, and all their friends,
None could take offence,
We had in-laws, too, (and outlaws!)
Is there any difference?
My job to set the table
And open up the wine,
The dining room looked splendid
When people came to dine.
Oh yes, I'd say that I could cook,
But I pray you, don't be deaf,
I really was assistant to
My wife, the master chef.

Unusual?

Is it so unusual
For a wife to be a lover?
With the same man, I mean,
And not with another.

And is it so unusual
To be a lover all her life?
And with the same man, I mean,
His lover and his wife.

The very best relationships,
Better than any other,
If he's lucky, a man can have
A wife who is his lover.

Perhaps it is unusual,
I don't really know,
But wife and lover you are to me,
From hereon to eternity,
Since so long ago.

Union Street, Aberdeen

You may not have been
To Aberdeen,
Or walked down Union Street,
But every time that I came home,
It seemed to me a treat.

When I left Dyce
Which was not very nice,
To catch the train to Leeds
I'd come to Aberdeen and Union Street,
For shops to suit my needs.

I remember buying you a headsquare,
On one journey back from there,
But the one I remember most,
Was the last time that I shopped there,
Before coming down the coast.

I left my kitbag in the doorway,
Of a jewellers in Union Street
And bought a broach for you to wear,
On my last trip down from Aberdeen,
To join my love so fair.

This modest broach that I brought back,
Was all I could afford,
But you have kept it all your life,
It was one that you adored.
Oh, how fast my heart did beat
At that jeweller's shop in Union Street.

Andalucia

Andalucia, castles in Spain
Reina Christina, let's go back again
The long beaches that stretch
North to Cadiz
The cut-outs of bulls
On the hills near Jerez
On past the wind farm
The sand stretches away
The simple white villages
Tourists keep away
No one around us but
The sea and the sand
The sun seems to shine
On this beautiful land
We climb the Giraldo
In sun-drenched Seville
Go to Granada
A dream to fulfil
Andalucia, castles in Spain
Beautiful white towns, lets go back again.

Poems for the POU

*The POU is the
Pulmonary Oncology Unit,
The lung cancer unit,
at Wythenshawe Hospital,
Manchester*

The POU

When you go to the POU
You know God has forsaken you.
No more happiness and laughter,
All that is left is the Hereafter.
No more blue skies, summer sun,
All the good times now are done.
When you go to the POU,
You know God has forsaken you.

You know that He's got other people,
To pray to Him beneath the steeple.
Other ones to sing His praise,
Not thinking that there may come days,
Days when they, like me and you,
Find themselves at the POU.
And when you go to the POU,
You know God has forsaken you.

That may be so, but you will find
That those who work there have in mind
To love, and help, and cherish you,
To do whatever they can do,
To fight the cancer, give you hope,
So you won't sit around and mope.
They'll do their damnedest, and it's true,
You'll find they've not forsaken you,
When you go to the POU.

The POU

At the POU
At Wythenshawe
However hard they'd strive
No patient ever quite pulled through
No patient stayed alive.

They did their best
With chemo
They tried every trick
Though loving care helped those there
They could not save the sick.

'Smiler' they called Jean
At the POU
'An inspiration,' someone said to me
Cheerful and elegant to the last
She never said, 'Why me?'

She was so very,
Very brave
Though she only had a while
Enchanting all around her
With her sparkling eyes and smile.

A strange place is
The POU
Death is everywhere
But the courage of those condemned
Inspires all who venture there.

Hope

When you go to the POU
They fill you full of dope
And although they say it's terminal
You still believe there's hope.

And when they give you chemo
They ask if you can cope
And if you take it in your stride
You still believe there's hope.

No one ever tells you
That it's time that you are buying
And that, ere long, it will run out
However hard you're trying.

But that's the way it goes
At the POU
The chemo gives a few more months
What else can you do?

They do their best to help you
They fill you full of dope
And although they say it's terminal
They still want you to hope.

The Board at the POU

Just inside the door that leads
From where people sit and wait all day,
To the wards and the treatment room,
And a few singles where the lucky stay,
Is a board.
It shows each name and where they are,
So that when you go, and have to wait,
You can visit those patients, now friends,
With this dread illness, you relate,
And give them what time you can afford.

You are now all in this club,
Of people terminally ill.
Yet love and friendship still persist,
You make of it what you will.
And on the board
Are names of every friend,
Not long known, but still as dear,
United by your suffering,
United by your fear
And you give them what time you can afford.

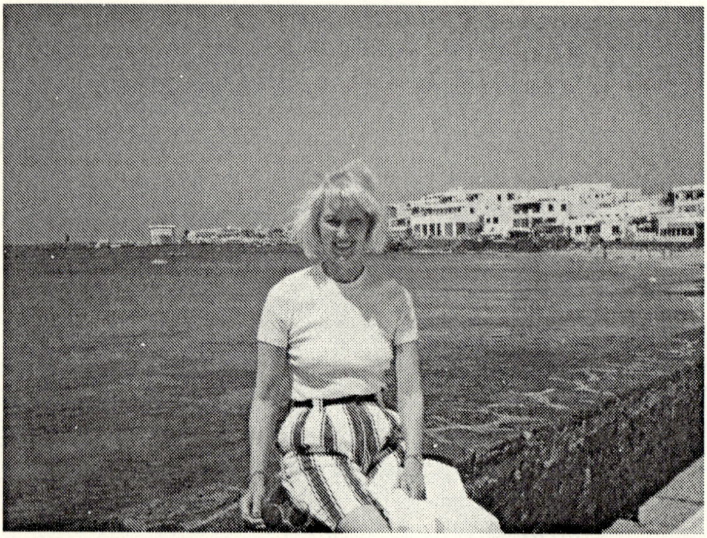

Lanzarote

We stroll along the front at Playa Blanca,
It is a warm Canaries' day,
The ferry lies off the shore at anchor,
On the beach we can see children at play.
Why can't we stay here forever? I think,
You look so lovely at my side,
Elegant, blonde, and beautiful,
For forty-one years you've been my bride.
Across the water is Fuerteventura.
We were there only two years before,
So happy then, not knowing what awaited,
Having no idea what lay in store.
       You're feeling better now, no chemo dope,
       You look so lovely, I can only hope.

Bill

Bill, I think that was his name,
Had lost all his hair.
A result of his chemo treatment,
Like the rest of those who were there.

Fighting this dreadful battle,
We all know can't be won,
Hoping to get a few more months,
What else can be done?

Bill had a sense of humour,
And so the ladies wouldn't be bored,
He'd got hold of some sample wigs,
And took them to their ward.

'Which do you think suits me?
The brown, the ginger or blond?'
And he pranced about the ladies' ward,
As in turn each wig he donned.

For just a few cheerful moments,
Each tired and weary eye
Lit up with fun and laughter,
Because of Bill,
A super guy.

Remember You Are Mine

'Be careful,' you used to say to me,
When I drove to Wilmslow for the wine.
'Remember the dark and twisting road,
And the Saturday night drivers,
Be careful, don't forget that you are mine.'

We used to treat ourselves,
On a winter's Saturday night.
Curl up by the tele, get some fish and chips and wine
Now that's what I call living,
When you're with the girl who's right,
'Be careful,' you said, 'don't forget it's Saturday night.'

Years later, when you went to the POU
It wasn't a Saturday night driver
Who parted me and you.
And after chemo treatment, as we went home for the night,
We'd call and get some fish and chips,
You were putting up a fight.
'Be careful,' I said, as we sat and drank red wine,
'Don't let the cancer beat you, love,
Remember, you are mine.'

Gemcitabine

Alice was the sister at the POU,
An Asian lady of modest build,
She was the one who saw to me and you,
The job was never better filled.

The chemo nurses were under her,
The auxiliaries who made the tea,
The bed-hunters from other wards,
'Twas her they had to see.

Heather was a consultant at the POU,
Second only to the Christies' Prof,
Her chemo recipes were on a board,
You could go and tick yours off.

Jean was met by Heather,
On our first visit there,
'I don't want any chemo,
If it makes me lose my hair.'

Heather said, 'Don't worry,
There's a trial drug on the scene,
You should keep most, or all your hair,
If you have Gemcitabine.'

We stayed the night, and they took tests,
'How long have I got?' asked Jean,
'The average is six months,' said Heather,
'But we'll try Gemcitabine.'

The months went by, and gradually
The X-rays did improve.
This was almost more than we dared hope,
Could they possibly cure my love?

Six months have gone, and the X-rays now
Are almost showing clean,
'Take a few months off,' said Heather,
Thank God for Gemcitabine.

So we went to Lanzarote,
Our hearts were full of hope
And Jean felt so much better,
No longer taking dope.

They said that it was terminal,
No cure had been seen,
Could it be Jean was the first
Cured by Gemcitabine?

Alas, only a few more weeks
Before events turned bad
The cancer came back in her legs,
No holidays now we had.

Back once more to the POU,
A downhill road from here
Alice, Heather, and the rest
Could not save my love so dear.

For a short while we were smiling,
I think what might have been,
If only that trial drug had worked,
Chemo Gemcitabine.

Alice was a sister
At the POU,
Heather a consultant there,
They tried everything they knew
To save my Jean, so fair.

Lamb Chops

Do you remember Dorothy, a widow?
Looked after by her son,
He cooked her favourite lamb chops.
You were in the next bed
To Dorothy, at the POU,
After you'd both had your ops.

Later we saw Dorothy and her son,
You had both gone for X-rays.
Now you both were in wheelchairs,
These were not happy days.

Yet I remember the laughter,
As we all sat and joked,
Dorothy, her son and you, all smiling,
What thoughts this provoked.

I guess Dorothy has gone, now.
Just like you my love,
But I hope you are both laughing,
In that place above.
      While Dorothy's son is still the tops
      Cooking their favourite lamb chops.

The Bed

'I want to go and buy a bed,'
I remember clearly what you said.
'One I can lie in when people come
To visit me when I'm at home.
One that looks both clean and new
When people visit me and you.
One that's just right, as I lie here,
As the months go by and the end draws near.
One that is fresh, and clean and new.
Oh, my darling, I love you.'

'Please don't talk about this bed.
It's very mention brings me dread.'
I remember clearly what you said.
'I want to go and buy a bed.'

'When my time comes, it's here I'll lie.
We cannot stop this happening,
My darling, please don't cry.'

An Inspiration

This young woman came to me.
She'd be about thirty-five,
An age when most of us,
Are glad to be alive.
      But she looked as though nought could entrance her,
      She'd just been told she had lung cancer.

Apparently her friends at work,
Had put some cash together,
So that she and her husband could holiday,
Enjoy some sunny weather.
      But she'd decided to stay at home,
      With loved ones near, take what might come.

We sat on seats and chatted away,
It was crowded there in the waiting hall,
'Your wife is just wonderful,' she said,
'An inspiration to us all.'
      And I saw Jean chat, and make her smile,
      In that no-hope place, the sun shone a while.

The Corridor

There is a long, long corridor that goes,
From the chest clinic to the X-ray department,
And needing an X-ray, everyone knows,
That this corridor is not level,
It has a hill right in the middle,
This corridor where everyone is sent.

You were very ill when we went to the clinic,
Once a month, like everybody there,
We went to see, was the chemo working,
And like many others, you were in a chair,
And I would wheel you to have an X-ray,
Please God, show the X-ray clear.

Yet although in this place we were despairing,
Though patients were so desperately ill,
And many, like you, had lung cancer,
A disease which we all knew would kill.
An Irish nurse would joke as she would weigh you,
Then off down the corridor we would go,
We would have some fun with the wheelchair,
Pushing hard as we went along the up side,
Then laughing and freewheeling down the low.

And as we came back we could see others,
Holding their X-rays to the light,
And we knew, before we ever saw the doctor,
Was it better?
Were you still in there with a fight?

The Waiting Room

There is a waiting room at Wythenshawe,
At the POU,
And usually there are ten or twenty there,
And there they wait.
In the morning they give blood samples,
Later see the doctor,
And then they have their chemo,
There is plenty of time for a debate.

There's a veranda outside the doors,
Of the POU,
For the eighty per cent of those
Who are there because they smoke.
And some shuffle out,
In dressing gown and slippers,
Sometimes in the snow.
If they couldn't have a cigarette they'd choke.

The carers fuss around the room
At the POU.
What comfort can they possibly give
To those waiting there?
The auxiliaries bring round the drinks,
I think we'll have beef tea.
We sit among the others, you and me,
It is very hard not to feel despair.

Moira

Moira and her husband
Sat in the waiting room,
Not a word was said
Her husband was out of work,
Her sister had MS,
And her diagnosis filled her with dread,
    And she was only thirty-four.

This was their first visit to the POU,
There were twenty or more waiting there.
A carer went to talk to them,
But they answered not,
What kind of experience has a carer got?
How can a carer care?
    When you are only thirty-four.

In a ladies ward, a few weeks later,
Moira was with Dorothy and Jean,
And an older lady, with a sense of humour.
They made Moira smile a little,
And I heard her chat.
For a little while she forgot her tumour.
    But she was only thirty-four.

It would be so good to be alive,
And get to thirty-five.

And now…

Winter

I don't care if it is Spring
Or Summer's coming on
For me it is still Winter
Now that you are gone.

Time

Do not smile at me, Time,
I have no room for you,
When I had paradise right here,
What, then, did you do?

When not a cloud was in the sky,
When all was bright and blue,
When not a worry crossed our minds,
What, then, did you do?

You sent me grief and sorrow,
You took away the sun,
You robbed me of my dearest love,
Oh, Time, what have you done?

Our Time

I have had my time
Whatever now occurs
And though not quite as long as mine
You, too, had yours.

We lived in good times
You, my love, and I
And though those days are now gone
We saw the sky.

No one can do more
Than you and I did then
We loved and lived life to the full
Scored ten out of ten.

I have had my time
Whatever now will be
It will not match those times when
You were with me.

If You Go Away

When, after many lovely years
Doctors confirmed our worst fears,
And you slipped away,
All had now gone wrong.
Other words came to me that May,
'If you go away on a summer's day,
They might as well take the sun away.'

Now there's nothing left for me to say
But the words of that song.

Waiting

I remember waiting for you
At the corner of South Drive.
You were only just eighteen,
It was good to be alive.
You were suddenly beside me,
Your blue eyes and your smile.
It was very clear to me that
My waiting was worthwhile.

I waited for you through the years,
In many different ways.
Whenever we were not together,
These were lonely days.
When I was out there working,
I was waiting to get home.
When there were other folks around,
I'd wait for you to be alone.

Since I first started waiting,
Nearly fifty years have flown.
And how wonderful it was for me,
To have you for my own.
But now my darling you are gone,
I alone survive.
If only I could wait for you,
At the corner of South Drive.

The Defining Moment

It is now almost fifty years
Since I first saw you.
What a long time ago it seems
Since I met you, girl of my dreams,
Looked into eyes of blue.

There are defining moments
As we go through life.
The biggest one that came my way
Was that most defining day,
When you became my wife.

I cannot now imagine
What my life would have been.
You were wonderful for me
As anyone who knows, can see,
When you came on the scene.

I sometimes sit and ponder,
Now all those years have gone.
How that one defining moment came.
You gave your love, and took my name,
And in my heart live on.

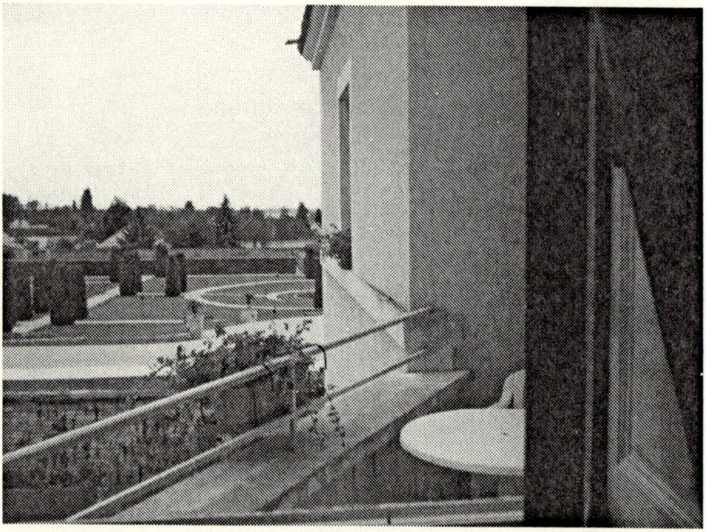

1953 and the Chateau de Gilly, 2002

I went on a moral leadership course,
From RAF Thornaby,
To Pulborough, near Arundel, in Sussex by the sea,
'Thank God I'm an atheist,' said Brian Thorpe,
As he waved Goodbye to me.

And when the course was over,
Before we went away,
We all were asked to write down,
If we could have our way
What things we'd like to happen to improve the day.

Only one thing I wanted,
And this was what I wrote,
'Only one thing could improve my stay,
Just one thing had my vote.
I'd like my love here with me,
Course leaders, please take note.

Fifty years have now gone by,
I'm alone at the Chateau, here,
I'd like my love back with me,
Course leader, can't You hear?'

The Dragonfly

I saw a dragonfly today,
Its body green and blue,
It flitted round the garden,
I wondered, was it you?

It was so very beautiful
As back and forth it flew,
Its colours shining in the sun,
I wondered, was it you?

You used to say that you'd come back,
After you'd passed away,
As an animal, a bird or flower,
You'd come back to me one day.

This dragonfly was elegant,
Its coat of green and blue
Shone brilliantly in the sun's rays,
I do hope it was you.

With You

I spent the night with you,
Although, of course, you were not here,
It's five years since you went away,
I still feel you near.

I spent the night with you,
With some lovely photographs,
Recalling so many good times,
The happiness and laughs.

I spent the night with you,
My memories are so clear,
It's almost as if, dear wife,
I still had you here.

I spent the night with you,
It will continue so,
Your love was everything to me,
How could I let you go?

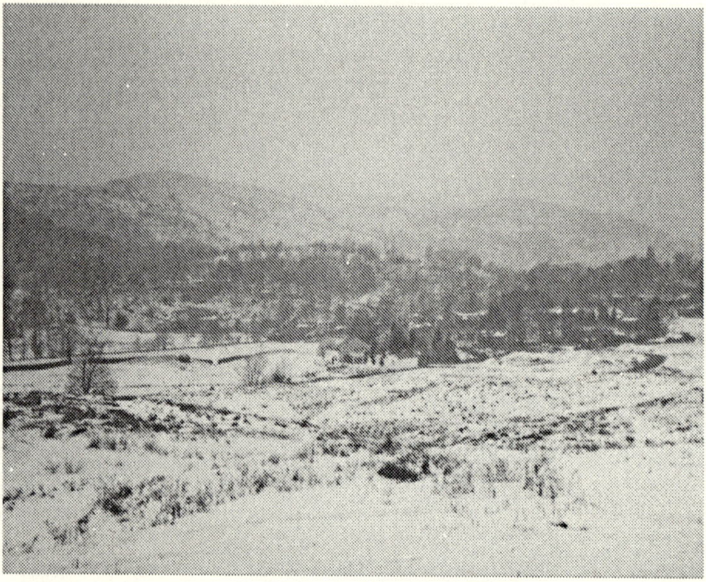

I Am With You

When the snow is on the ground,
And the night is dark and long,
When there's no one else around,
You shall hear my song.

When the sky is dull and grey,
And the hilltops all are bare,
Ignore what people say,
I shall be there.

You may not see my eyes smile,
You may not hear my voice,
But I am with you all the while,
My heart gives me no choice.

Life's ending does not matter,
Whatever people say,
Ignore their idle chatter,
I am with you every day.

Printed in the United Kingdom
by Lightning Source UK Ltd.
9654500001B/91-140